▪ PICTURE ▪ POCKET ▪

DINOSAURS

Series editor: Jackie Gaff
Series designer: Ben White Associates
Cover design: Terry Woodley
Cover illustration: Eric Robson/Garden Studio
Illustrations by: Chris Forsey (pp. 30–1),
Haywood Art Group (pp. 4–5, 8–9), Bernard Long/
Temple Rogers (pp. 22–5, 34–5, 50–1, 56–7, 74–7,
88–9), Kevin Maddison (pp. 36–7, 48–9, 58–61,
72–3), Alan Male/Linden Artists (pp. 10–17, 32–3,
40–3, 52–3, 62–3, 68–71), Tony Morris/Linda
Rogers Associates (pp. 6–7, 18–21, 26–9, 38–9,
44–7, 54–5, 64–7, 78–87).

Kingfisher Books, Grisewood & Dempsey Ltd,
Elsley House, 24–30 Great Titchfield Street,
London W1P 7AD

First published in 1991 by Kingfisher Books

BRITISH LIBRARY CATALOGUING IN PUBLICATION DATA
Benton, Michael 1939–
   Dinosaurs
   1. Dinosaurs
   I. Title II. Series
567.91

ISBN 0 86272 721 9

Phototypeset by Southern Positives and
Negatives (SPAN), Lingfield, Surrey.
Printed in Hong Kong

DINOSAURS

MICHAEL BENTON

Kingfisher Books

CONTENTS

PREHISTORIC LIFE

If you could travel millions of years back in time you'd find it difficult to recognize any of the animals and plants around you – most of them were quite unlike anything alive on Earth today. You'd probably find life frightening as well as strange, since you'd only reach to the knees of many animals!

Dunkleosteus (1) was a fish as big as a bus. Dryopithecus (2) was a type of ape. Pteranodon (3) was a flying relative of the dinosaurs. Apatosaurus (4) and Iguanodon (5) were large plant-eating dinosaurs. The dinosaur Compsognathus (6) was the size of a hen. Baluchitherium (7) was an early rhinoceros, Mammuthus (8) was an early elephant, and Archaeopteryx (9) was an early form of bird. The first dragonflies (10) were as big as seagulls!

You are tiny (11) in comparison to most of these prehistoric animals.

Most of these unusual animals lived well before our human ancestors appeared on Earth 2 million years ago. We call the story of ancient life prehistory, or 'before history'. The time we call history began about 5000 years ago, when writing was invented and people were able to record events.

When Did Life Begin?

When the Earth formed about 4600 million years ago, it was a boiling hot mass of molten rock – rather like lava from an erupting volcano. It was far too hot for anything to live, and another 1100 million years passed before the Earth was cool enough for the oceans to form. About 100 million years after that, the first living things appeared in the water. These were bacteria – microscopic living things, more like plants than animals, but related to both.

AGES OF TIME

MYA = million years ago

Scientists divide prehistory into periods that cover millions of years.

MYA	
2	Pleistocene – humans
5	Pliocene – 1st cattle
24	Miocene – 1st apes & mice
37	Oligocene – 1st dogs & cats
58	Eocene – 1st horses & elephants
65	Palaeocene – mammals take over
144	Cretaceous – 1st flowers
208	Jurassic – dinosaurs rule
245	Triassic – 1st dinosaurs & mammals
286	Permian – many animals die out
360	Carboniferous – 1st reptiles
408	Devonian – 1st amphibians & insects
438	Silurian – 1st land plants
505	Ordovician – 1st starfish
570	Cambrian – 1st fish & shellfish
4600	Precambrian – life begins in the oceans

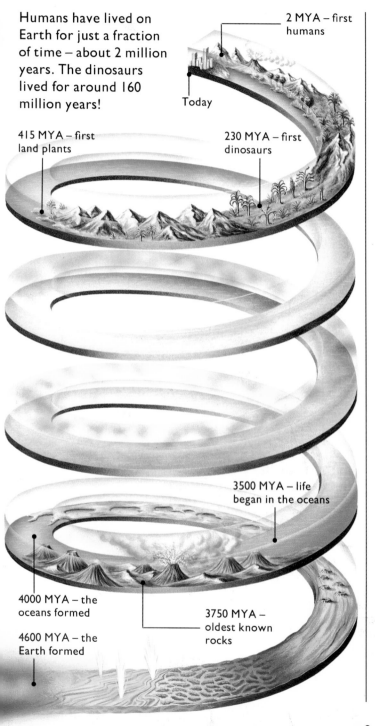

Humans have lived on Earth for just a fraction of time – about 2 million years. The dinosaurs lived for around 160 million years!

2 MYA – first humans

Today

415 MYA – first land plants

230 MYA – first dinosaurs

3500 MYA – life began in the oceans

4000 MYA – the oceans formed

3750 MYA – oldest known rocks

4600 MYA – the Earth formed

Life in the Ancient Seas

The countless different species, or kinds, of animals and plants that live on Earth today all developed from the first simple life forms that appeared in the oceans 3500 million years ago. Over a very long time, these early life forms developed into new plant and animal species. This slow process of change and development in living things is called evolution.

During Cambrian times (570–505 million years ago), many new groups of animals evolved in the oceans. They included the first animals to grow a tough outer shell – the ancestors of modern shellfish.

Pikaia may have been our earliest ancestor! It was a tiny fish-like creature.

Marella had a lot of legs and a jointed hard outer shell. It grew to be about 10 mm long.

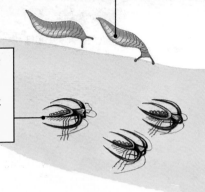

FOSSIL FACT FILE

Scientists have learnt about prehistoric life by studying fossils – the remains of ancient life, often turned to stone. Most fossils formed in water, after a dead plant or animal had sunk to the bottom of a lake or sea. Usually, the soft parts of the plant or animal rotted away, leaving the hard parts to be covered by sand or mud. Over hundreds of thousands of years this hardened into rock, with the shape of the plant or animal preserved inside it as a fossil.

At 11 cm long, Anomalocaris was the largest meat-eater of its day. It had strong jaws to crush its food with.

Hallucigenia was the strangest of the Cambrian sea animals. It had seven tube-like mouths running down its back!

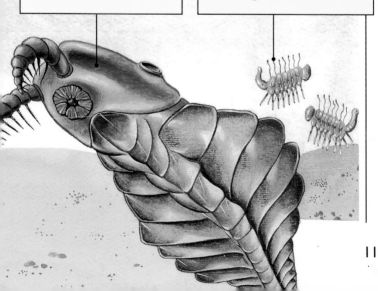

11

The Age of Fish

The first fish appeared in Cambrian times. They were small and eel-like, and they were the first animals to have a backbone. These early fish didn't have jaws, though – they sucked up food from the mud on the sea or lake floor. Fish with jaws had evolved by Devonian times (408–360 million years ago).

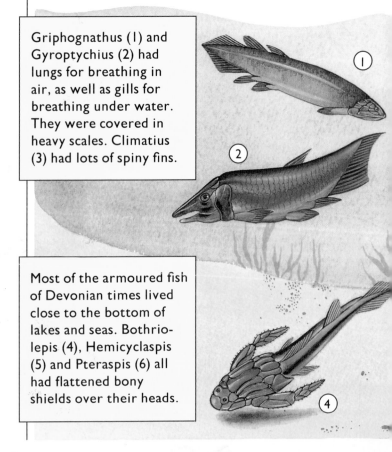

Griphognathus (1) and Gyroptychius (2) had lungs for breathing in air, as well as gills for breathing under water. They were covered in heavy scales. Climatius (3) had lots of spiny fins.

Most of the armoured fish of Devonian times lived close to the bottom of lakes and seas. Bothrio-lepis (4), Hemicyclaspis (5) and Pteraspis (6) all had flattened bony shields over their heads.

The Devonian period is sometimes called the Age of Fish, because by this time such a wide variety of different fish were living in the seas and lakes. Some of these Devonian fish were 9-metre-long monsters, so it's no wonder that many smaller fish developed a protective coat of bony 'armour'!

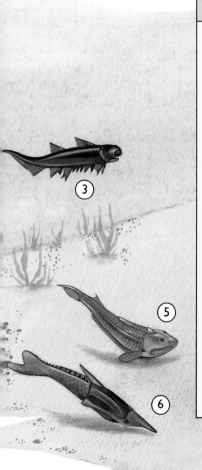

Life on Dry Land

One of the new Devonian fish groups made a remarkable move about 400 million years ago – on to dry land! The fish were probably tempted on shore by the extra food supplies offered by the new land plants and small creepy-crawly insects. Those unusual fish had to deal with some new problems, though.

In many ways life on land is more difficult than in the water. Bodies weigh more on land, so land animals need a

FACT FILE

Amphibians live in water and on land – the word amphibian means 'leading a double life'.

Amphibians lay soft jelly-like eggs in water. The eggs hatch into fish-like tadpoles which develop legs and move on to the land as they grow into adults.

During Carboniferous times (360–286 million years ago), much of the land was covered with forests of giant trees with long fern-like leaves.

firm skeleton to support their bodies, and strong leg muscles so they can move about. Over time, the fleshy fins of the first fish to move on land became legs, and a new group of animals, the amphibians, had evolved.

Carboniferous forests were full of insect life – Arthropleura (1) was a 2-metre-long millipede! Early amphibians included the fish-eater Eogyrinus (2) and the tadpole-like Branchiosaurus (3). Diplocaulus (4) was one of the strangest-looking amphibians. It had a wide boomerang-shaped head.

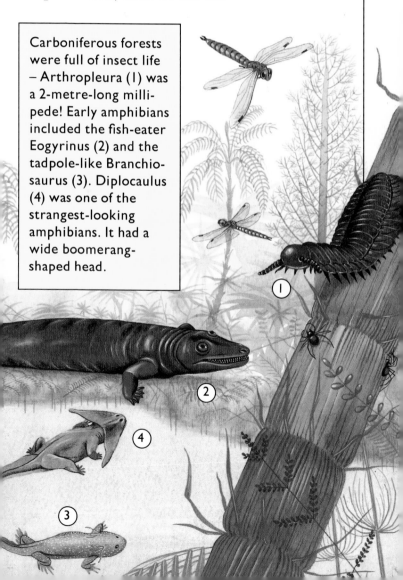

The Rise of Reptiles

The next new animals to appear were reptiles, the ancestors of modern lizards, snakes and turtles. Unlike amphibians, which have to live near water to lay their eggs and keep their skins moist, reptiles have waterproof skins and can live in hot dry places such as deserts. Because of this, many more reptiles than amphibians survived when the Earth's

Eryops was one of the few amphibibians that could survive in the dry climate of Permian times.

The reptile Varano-saurus grew to be 3 metres long – it was as big as a family car!

climate became hotter and drier at the beginning of the Permian period (286 million years ago).

The first reptiles were small insect-eaters. Soon, though, they branched out into many different species. The new reptiles included meat-eaters and plant-eaters – some were mouse-sized, but others were as big as rhinoceroses!

The sail-backs of reptiles like Dimetrodon were used to take in the Sun's heat when the animals were cold and to give heat off when they were hot.

FACT FILE

Unlike amphibians, reptiles lay their eggs on land. Reptiles' eggs are protected from drying out by their shells, and the babies that hatch out look like the adults, only smaller. Modern reptiles include lizards, snakes crocodiles and turtles.

Edaphosaurus was another large sail-backed reptile. It was a plant-eater.

Enter the Dinosaurs

The first dinosaurs appeared on Earth towards the end of the Triassic period (245–208 million years ago). Their ancestors were in a reptile group called the archosaurs, or 'ruling reptiles'.

The archosaurs were meat-eaters, and during Triassic times they evolved into two main groups. One group eventually gave rise to crocodiles. The other developed into the dinosaurs and the pterosaurs, which were flying reptiles. The dinosaurs were the most successful animals ever to have lived on Earth – they ruled for 160 million years!

Procompsognathus was one of the earliest dinosaurs. It was small and speedy and it fed on lizards and frogs.

By the late Triassic most plants were still fern-like. There were pine-like conifer trees, but no flowers or grass.

Eudimorphodon was the first pterosaur. It was the size of a seagull and it ate insects, catching them in flight.

Plateosaurus was the first large plant-eating dinosaur. It was about 8 metres long, and it fed on leaves from tall trees.

Protosuchus was an early type of crocodile which lived on land as well as in the water. It was about a metre long.

19

Dinosaurs Rule

During Jurassic times (208–144 million years ago) the dinosaurs spread worldwide and became the most successful animal group on land. Many new dinosaur species had developed since the Triassic. Gigantic plant-eaters such as Brachiosaurus and Diplodocus had evolved from Plateosaurus – they were more than 20 metres long and taller than a four-storey house! There were large meat-eaters, too – Allosaurus was the size of a bus, for example.

Turtles (1) are reptiles that have changed little since they first appeared in Triassic times. Jurassic dinosaurs included the meat-eater Elaphrosaurus (2) and the plant-eater Dryosaurus (3). About 3-4 metres long, they could move quickly on their strong back legs. Rhamphorhynchus (4) was a pterosaur.

The climate was warm in Jurassic times, but it was wetter than it had been in the Triassic. Plants thrived in the damp and the warmth.

Morganucodon (right) was one of the first mammals. This group appeared on Earth in the late Triassic, at about the same time as the early dinosaurs. Unlike other animals, mammals give birth to live young which feed on milk made in the mother's body.

The lush plant life of the Jurassic included thick forests of tall conifer trees, as well as ferns and long feathery horsetails. Dinosaurs needed strong teeth to eat these tough plants.

21

Underwater Reptiles

As the age of dinosaurs began, some reptiles evolved wings and took to the air as pterosaurs, while others went back to the water. There were two main groups of sea-going reptiles. Plesiosaurs had long necks and sharp teeth. Most species fed on fish, but there were giant plesiosaurs that ate small sea reptiles such as turtles as well as fish.

Cryptocleidus was a medium-sized plesiosaur, about 3 metres long. It ate fish, catching them with its sharp teeth and swallowing them whole.

Jurassic seas teemed with fish and shellfish, as well as all sorts of reptiles.

Ichthyosaurs looked rather like dolphins do today. They were so well suited to life in the water that they could no longer go on land, even to lay eggs. Fossils show us that ichthyosaur mothers kept their eggs inside their bodies until the babies hatched out of them. The mothers then gave birth to live young in the water.

As its name suggests, Ichthyosaurus was an ichthyosaur. It lived near the water surface and ate fish and shellfish.

Metriorhynchus was a 2-metre-long sea crocodile whose tail had grown a fish-like fin.

Flying Reptiles

The skies above the dinosaur lands were filled with the flapping leathery wings of the flying reptiles we call pterosaurs. Most pterosaurs were the size of seagulls, but some were bigger than any bird alive today. The largest pterosaur, Quetzalcoatlus, had a wingspan that measured an amazing 12 metres – the same as that of a small aircraft!

FACT FILE

Birds lay hard-shelled eggs – reptiles' eggs are leathery. Birds have beaks instead of jaws and teeth. Their front limbs are wings, and birds have feathers!

Like most pterosaurs, Dimorphodon was the same size as a seagull today. Each wing was supported inside by very long finger bones.

Dimorphodon's large beak was lined with teeth. It may have been used for scooping fish and shellfish from shallow water.

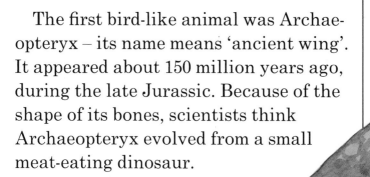

The first bird-like animal was Archaeopteryx – its name means 'ancient wing'. It appeared about 150 million years ago, during the late Jurassic. Because of the shape of its bones, scientists think Archaeopteryx evolved from a small meat-eating dinosaur.

Archaeopteryx was only the size of a modern pigeon. Its body and wings were covered in feathers, so it could probably fly. Unlike modern birds, however, Archaeopteryx had claws on the end of its wings and teeth inside its beak-like mouth.

The First Flowers

It may seem hard to imagine a time without flowers, but until Cretaceous times (144–65 million years ago) there weren't any flowering plants. Among the first to appear were roses and primulas, as well as ash, fig, magnolia, maple, oak, sycamore and willow trees.

The two main dinosaur groups in Cretaceous times were plant-eaters. The ornithopods walked on two legs, and many of them had head-crests and mouths shaped like ducks' bills. The ceratopsians walked on all fours and had fierce sets of horns on their heads.

Corythosaurus was a typical ornithopod, with a crest and a duckbill. These dinosaurs' crests were hollow and joined to the nostrils by tubes — they may have been used to make honking sounds.

By Cretaceous times, birds no longer had teeth or wing-claws. Many were fish-eaters and looked more like modern bird species.

Triceratops was a large ceratopsian which used its horns to protect itself against the fierce meat-eaters of its time.

The first snakes came on the scene during Cretaceous times. They were meat-eaters, like the snakes of today.

A Prehistoric Puzzle

All the dinosaurs died out about 65 million years ago, but no one knows exactly why. The Earth's climate grew cooler at about this time, and some people think it was too cold for the dinosaurs to survive.

A more dramatic idea is that the Earth was hit by giant rocks from outer Space. The force of their landing threw up a huge dust cloud which blacked out the Sun. Plants can't live without sunlight. When the plants died, first the plant-eating dinosaurs starved to death, then the meat-eaters.

No one knows exactly why the dinosaurs vanished 65 million years ago – and why when they died out, birds and other animals survived.

EXTINCTION FACT FILE

Many other creatures died out at the end of the Cretaceous. In addition to the dinosaurs, the ichthyosaurs, plesiosaurs and pterosaurs all vanished from the Earth forever.

The lucky survivors included most plant and fish species, as well as snails, insects, crabs, frogs, lizards, snakes, crocodiles, turtles, sharks, birds and the early mammals.

EGG THIEVES?

Perhaps other animals ate the dinosaurs' eggs – but could all of their eggs have been eaten in all parts of the world?

FOOD POISONING?

Perhaps the flowering plants poisoned the dinosaurs – but these plants had already been around for 50 million years!

AIR POLLUTION?

Perhaps the dinosaurs were poisoned by gases from erupting volcanoes – but why weren't all the other animals poisoned?

DINOSAURS A-Z

The first dinosaur fossils were collected in England in the 1800s, often at the foot of cliffs or in old quarries. Since then, hundreds of different dinosaurs have been found. A guide to some of the most interesting dinosaurs follows in the next section of this book.

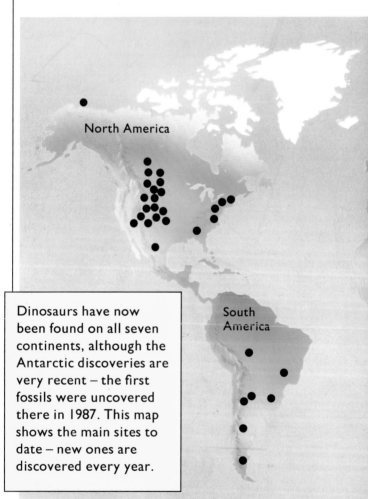

North America

South America

Dinosaurs have now been found on all seven continents, although the Antarctic discoveries are very recent – the first fossils were uncovered there in 1987. This map shows the main sites to date – new ones are discovered every year.

Antarctica

DINOSAUR FACT FILES

Each dinosaur has a fact file which tells you what its name means and how to say it.

Dinosaurs are sometimes named after the person who found them or the place where they were first discovered. Many names include the word *saurus*, which means 'reptile'.

The fact files also tell you where dinosaurs have been found and how big they were. The capital letter tells you when the dinosaur lived:

T = Triassic (245–208 million years ago)
J = Jurassic (208–144 million years ago)
C = Cretaceous (144–65 million years ago)

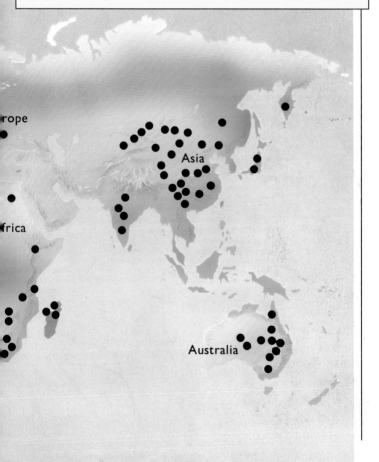

rope

Asia

frica

Australia

Acanthopholis

Acanthopholis was one of the earliest armoured dinosaurs. Its back was covered with bony plates which were set into its skin, and some of the plates had spikes sticking out of them. This armour protected Acanthopholis from the deadly jaws of meat-eating dinosaurs.

The protective layer of armour was made from bone which grew within the skin. It formed a very hard covering for the back, neck and tail.

Acanthopholis was a plant-eater. It had a narrower head than its relative Ankylosaurus.

FACT FILE

- a-KAN-tho-FOLE-is
- 'Spine bearer'
- Lived in southern England

5.5m

Allosaurus

This fierce meat-eater fed on the plant-eating dinosaurs of its time such as Dryosaurus and Stegosaurus. Its strong arms and claws were probably used to catch small animals, while its jaws were powerful enough to break the bones of its unlucky victims.

FACT FILE

- al-oh-SAW-rus
- 'Strange reptile'
- Lived in North America

12m

Its teeth were long and curved, and edged with a zig-zag pattern to help tear into flesh.

Its hind legs were strong enough to support its weight, so Allosaurus could walk upright while using its front arms to grasp and tear food.

Anatosaurus

Anatosaurus was a duckbilled dinosaur which was related to Corythosaurus and Parasaurolophus. Some Anatosaurus fossils have been found with pieces of dried skin attached to the fingers. These show that Anatosaurus probably had webbed fingers, like a duck's, and may have been able to swim.

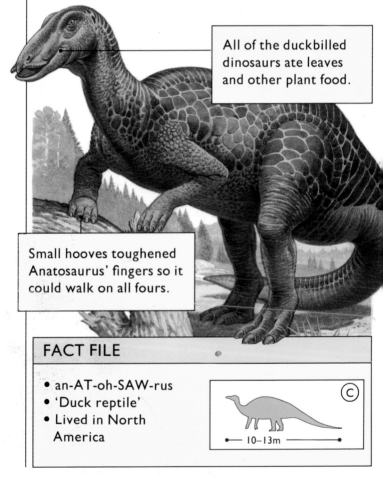

All of the duckbilled dinosaurs ate leaves and other plant food.

Small hooves toughened Anatosaurus' fingers so it could walk on all fours.

FACT FILE

- an-AT-oh-SAW-rus
- 'Duck reptile'
- Lived in North America

10–13m

Ankylosaurus

The armoured dinosaurs were often very large, and Ankylosaurus was one of the largest – as big and heavy as a modern army tank! It was a plant-eater, and the bony plates set in the skin of its head, back and tail helped to protect it from attack by meat-eaters. It also had a powerful club at the end of its tail.

FACT FILE

- an-KY-low-SAW-rus
- 'Stiff reptile'
- Lived in North America

10–17m

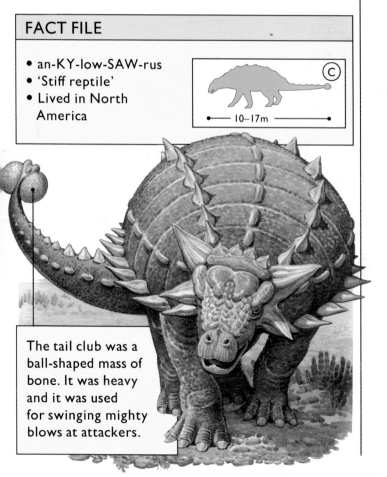

The tail club was a ball-shaped mass of bone. It was heavy and it was used for swinging mighty blows at attackers.

Apatosaurus

Apatosaurus was a huge plant-eater and it belonged to a group that included the gigantic Diplodocus and Brachiosaurus. Scientists once thought that these plant-eaters must have lived in lakes, because they were so big that they needed the water to support their weight. We now know that they lived on land.

Apatosaurus ate leaves from tall trees. Its head was fairly small because it wasn't a meat-eater and it didn't need big powerful jaws.

- a-PAT-oh-SAW-rus
- 'Deceptive reptile'
- Lived in North America

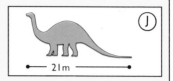

— 21m —

The heyday of Apatosaurus and the other giant plant-eating dinosaurs was 150 million years ago.

The tail made up half the body length. It may have been used like a whip to scare off attackers.

Baryonyx

In 1983 a huge 30-centimetre-long claw was found in southern England. Soon the rest of the skeleton had been dug up and the new dinosaur was named Baryonyx. So far, only one Baryonyx skeleton has been found. Surprisingly, for a land animal, the dinosaur's stomach had fish scales in it. This probably means that Baryonyx ate fish. It may have used its enormous claw to hook fish out of the water.

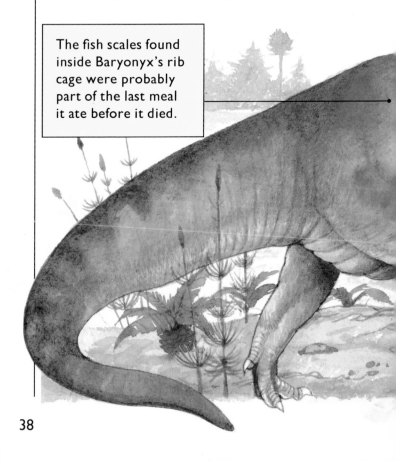

The fish scales found inside Baryonyx's rib cage were probably part of the last meal it ate before it died.

FACT FILE

- BAR-ee-ON-ix
- 'Heavy claw'
- Lived in southern England

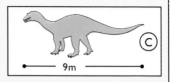

9m

Its crocodile-like head and small jaws also suggest that Baryonyx ate fish.

Scientists haven't yet discovered whether Baryonyx's claw was on its hand or its foot.

Brachiosaurus

Brachiosaurus was the tallest dinosaur of all. It was 12 metres high – if it were alive today it would be able to peer over a four-storey building! Scientists have discovered bones of dinosaurs that may have been taller, but until they find a complete new skeleton, Brachiosaurus holds the record.

FACT FILE

- BRACK-ee-oh-SAW-rus
- 'Arm reptile'
- Lived in N. America & eastern Africa

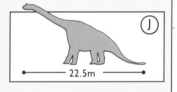

22.5m

Brachiosaurus' long neck only had 14 bones in it. Each bone was nearly half a metre long.

Ceratosaurus

Ceratosaurus was a meat-eater and may have hunted in groups, attacking larger animals such as Brachiosaurus. It also went after smaller prey on its own. Ceratosaurus had a low crest on the top of its skull which looked rather like a horn. It was actually made of bone and it was covered with skin.

Scientists believe that males attacked each other with their nose 'horns' when they fought over a mate.

FACT FILE

- SER-a-toe-SAW-rus
- 'Horned reptile'
- Lived in North America

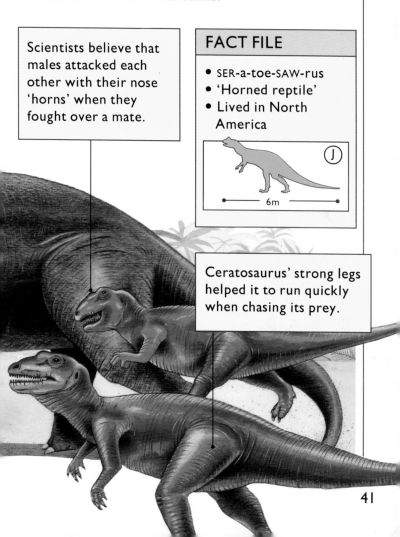

6m

J

Ceratosaurus' strong legs helped it to run quickly when chasing its prey.

Cetiosaurus

Cetiosaurus was one of the earliest of the big plant-eaters – it was an ancestor of Apatosaurus and Brachiosaurus. Huge bones from the backbone were first found in 1841, but a complete skeleton wasn't found until 1979.

Cetiosaurus was named in 1841, the year the word 'dinosaur' was invented by Sir Richard Owen.

FACT FILE

- SEET-ee-oh-SAW-rus
- 'Whale reptile'
- Lived in Europe & North Africa

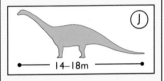

14–18m

The spoon-shaped teeth weren't very sharp. They were only useful for chomping on soft plants.

Coelophysis

Scientists think that Coelophysis was the first dinosaur to appear on Earth – it lived about 225 million years ago. In 1947, dozens of Coelophysis skeletons were found in a layer of rock in New Mexico, USA. These show that Coelophysis sometimes ate its own young!

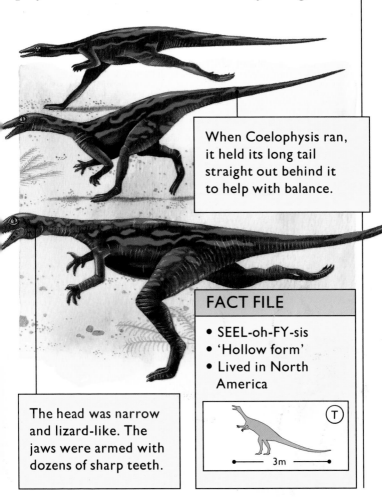

When Coelophysis ran, it held its long tail straight out behind it to help with balance.

The head was narrow and lizard-like. The jaws were armed with dozens of sharp teeth.

FACT FILE

- SEEL-oh-FY-sis
- 'Hollow form'
- Lived in North America

3m

Coelurus

Coelurus was a small meat-eater which lived in North America, under the feet of the giant plant-eaters Apatosaurus and Brachiosaurus. Its head was small and light, and its large eyes gave it sharp eyesight for hunting down its prey. Coelurus probably fed on small lizards and mammals, as well as on other dinosaurs' eggs.

Coelurus' lightweight body is typical of an animal that hunts and chases its prey.

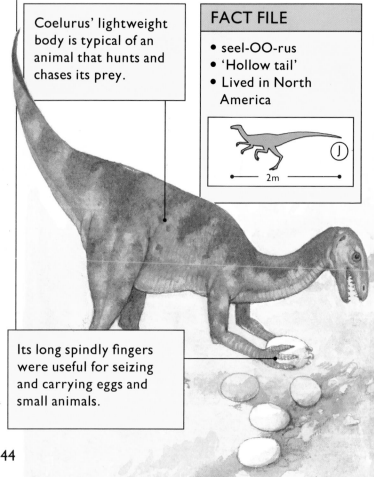

2m

J

Its long spindly fingers were useful for seizing and carrying eggs and small animals.

Compsognathus

Compsognathus is the smallest dinosaur yet discovered – its body was no larger than a turkey's! Its skeleton is known in beautiful detail because its tiny bones were turned to fossils in very fine mud. Even its last meal was preserved – a lizard which was so big and fat that Compsognathus may have choked to death trying to eat it!

FACT FILE

- komp-SOG-nath-us
- 'Pretty jaw'
- Lived in western Europe

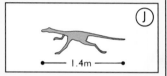

1.4m

Compsognathus was a fast runner, with thin legs and bird-like feet and toes.

Holding its long thin tail out behind it helped Compsognathus to keep its balance when running.

Corythosaurus

Corythosaurus was another duckbilled dinosaur. Its body looked similar to that of Anatosaurus, but Corythosaurus had a crest on top of its head. The crest varied in size. An adult male's was the size and shape of half a dinner plate. A female's crest was smaller than a male's, while a baby Corythosaurus barely had a crest at all.

FACT FILE

- ko-RITH-oh-SAW-rus
- 'Helmeted reptile'
- Lived in North America

Ⓒ

10m

Duckbills probably lived in family groups – small and large ones are found together.

The duckbills' crests weren't solid bone – breathing tubes ran from the mouth, up the crest and down to the nose. The crests may have used for honking.

Deinonychus

Deinonychus was the most exciting dinosaur discovery of the 1960s. It had a long and very sharp curved claw on one toe of each foot. Each of its three fingers also had a sharp claw. It attacked by kicking at its victim's belly with its sharp toe claw and slashing with its lethal finger claws.

The tail was stiffened by bony rods. Deinonychus used its tail to balance its body when slashing.

FACT FILE

- DIE-no-NIKE-us
- 'Terrible claw'
- Lived in North America

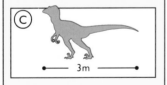

ⓒ

3m

Deinonychus flicked its long slashing claw up out of the way when running, and swung it down again when attacking its prey.

Diplodocus

Brachiosaurus may have been the tallest dinosaur, but its relative Diplodocus wins the prize for being the longest! The longest complete Diplodocus skeleton yet discovered measures 27 metres from its nose to the tip of its tail – about the same as seven cars parked end to end!

Like Apatosaurus, Diplodocus could swing its tail from side to side like a whip to scare attackers.

FACT FILE

- dip-LOD-oh-kus
- 'Double beam'
- Lived in North America

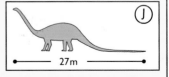

27m

Dryosaurus

Dryosaurus lived about 150 million years ago, during the late Jurassic, and was an ancestor of the duckbilled dinosaurs. It was a plant-eater, with teeth that were sharp enough to cut through twigs as well as leaves. Its hands were strong and could be used for gathering food.

FACT FILE

- DRY-oh-SAW-rus
- 'Oak reptile'
- Lived in eastern Africa & N. America

Ⓙ

3–4m

The shape of its jaw tells us that Dryosaurus had large fleshy cheeks. They were used to hold food while chewing.

Like many other dinosaurs, and most fast-running animals, Dryosaurus walked and ran on its toes.

Fabrosaurus

This dinosaur was another early plant-eater. Like Dryosaurus, it walked on its hind legs. It also had strong arms and hands, and its teeth were specially shaped for chewing up plants. But Fabrosaurus wasn't common, and only one complete skeleton has been found by scientists to date.

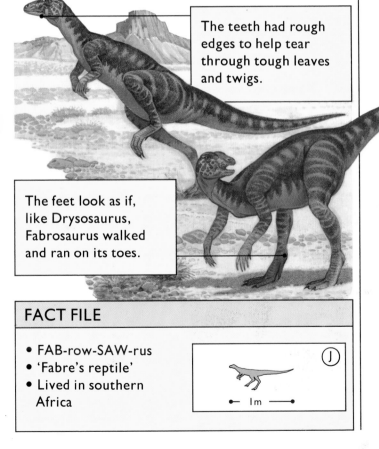

The teeth had rough edges to help tear through tough leaves and twigs.

The feet look as if, like Drysosaurus, Fabrosaurus walked and ran on its toes.

FACT FILE

- FAB-row-SAW-rus
- 'Fabre's reptile'
- Lived in southern Africa

J

← 1m →

Hypsilophodon

Hypsilophodon was a small plant-eating dinosaur which probably lived in herds. At one time scientists thought that it perched in trees to feed on leaves. But more recent fossil discoveries have shown that its feet were the wrong shape for grasping branches!

FACT FILE

- hip-see-LOAF-oh-don
- 'High-ridged tooth'
- Lived in southern England

2m

Hypsilophodon was the antelope of its day, with very long thin back legs which helped it to run fast.

The front of Hypsilophodon's jaw had bony pads (like a sheep's). Its chewing teeth were at the back of its mouth.

Iguanodon

Iguanodon lived 120 million years ago, side-by-side with Hypsilophodon in the warm forests of southern England. Iguanodon was more widespread than Hypsilophodon, though, and its fossils have been found in many countries, from Europe to North Africa and Asia.

Fossilized skin is rare, but Iguanodon fossils show that its skin was smooth and scaly.

FACT FILE

- ig-WA-no-don
- 'Iguana tooth'
- Europe, N. Africa, N. Asia & N. America

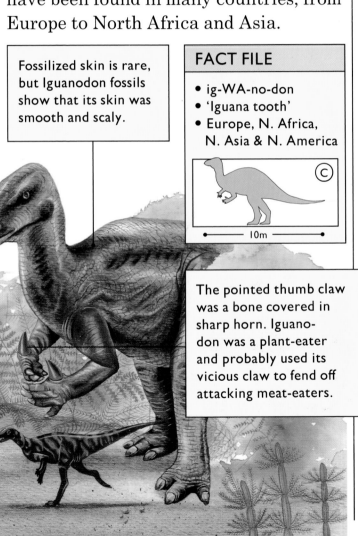

10m

The pointed thumb claw was a bone covered in sharp horn. Iguanodon was a plant-eater and probably used its vicious claw to fend off attacking meat-eaters.

Kentrosaurus

Kentrosaurus lived in eastern Africa at the same time as its relative Stego-saurus lived in North America. In some ways the two dinosaurs looked similar, but Kentrosaurus was less than half the size of Stegosaurus. It also had different kinds of spines to protect its body from attack by meat-eaters.

The long spine on its hip stuck out sideways, giving Kentrosaurus extra pro-tection from attackers.

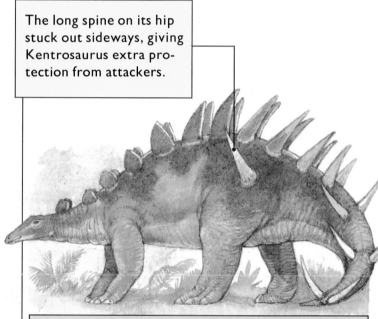

FACT FILE

- KEN-tro-SAW-rus
- 'Pointed reptile'
- Lived in eastern Africa

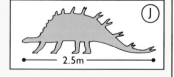

2.5m

Lambeosaurus

This large duckbilled dinosaur had a very unusual crest, quite different in shape from the rounded crest of its relative Corythosaurus. Some Lambeosaurus dinosaurs also had a spine that stuck out from the back of their heads.

Lambeosaurus crests came in all shapes and sizes – some were high, others were low. Some dinosaurs had the extra spine, others didn't!

Lambeosaurus was a plant-eater and its jaws were lined with rows of grinding teeth.

Maiasaura

Maiasaura was found only recently – in 1979. Because its skeleton was discovered close to its young and to nests full of eggs, scientists were able to uncover a lot of information about the way its young hatched and grew. We now know that Maiasaura cared for its young and came back to nest in the same place year after year.

The mother dug the nest out of a mound of earth. She then laid the eggs and covered them with soil.

The eggs hatched after a few weeks in the warm soil, and tiny baby dinosaurs crept out.

The mother dinosaur stayed near the nest. She helped the babies to find food because they couldn't wander far at first.

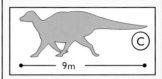

Megalosaurus

Megalosaurus was the first dinosaur to be named – in 1824. In fact, a book published in 1676 tells us that a bone of Megalosaurus had been found, but no one knew what it was. People thought it was a giant human bone! After more bones and teeth were found in the early 1800s, scientists realized that they belonged to a large meat-eating reptile.

The teeth had long roots to fix them deep in the jaw bone. The tiny sharp zigzags along the teeth edges are like those on the blade of a steak knife.

FACT FILE

- MEG-a-low-SAW-rus
- 'Great reptile'
- Lived in Europe & North Africa

9m

J

Muttaburrasaurus

Muttaburrasaurus is an Australian relative of Iguanodon. Other members of the Iguanodon family have been found in Africa, Asia, Europe and North America, and the discovery of Muttaburrasaurus in 1981 proved that the group once lived worldwide.

The bump on the head may have been used in head-butting contests between males.

FACT FILE

- MUT-a-BUR-a-saw-rus
- 'Muttaburra reptile'
- Lived in north-eastern Australia

© 7m

Scientists discovered small round bony plates on the dinosaur's body. They think that these may have formed a type of light body armour.

Ornithomimus

Ornithomimus was an unusual meat-eater – it had no teeth, just a horny beak covering its narrow jaws. Odd as this may seem, modern meat-eaters such as vultures and eagles also manage without teeth. Although Ornithomimus could grow to be 4 metres long and 2 metres tall, it probably weighed less than a human adult does today.

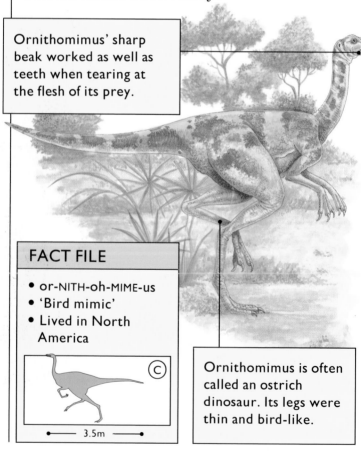

Ornithomimus' sharp beak worked as well as teeth when tearing at the flesh of its prey.

FACT FILE

- or-NITH-oh-MIME-us
- 'Bird mimic'
- Lived in North America

©

3.5m

Ornithomimus is often called an ostrich dinosaur. Its legs were thin and bird-like.

Ouranosaurus

Unlike its relative Iguanodon, Ourano-saurus had a remarkable sail-like crest. This crest allowed Ouranosaurus to lose heat into the outside air when it was hot, or to take in heat from the Sun when it was cold.

Head fossils show that Ouranosaurus' jaws moved sideways when it chewed food.

FACT FILE

- oo-RAN-oh-SAW-rus
- 'Brave reptile'
- Lived in north-western Africa

7m

Ouranosaurus' sail-like crest helped it to control its body temperature.

Pachycephalosaurus

Pachycephalosaurus was a large dinosaur with an incredibly thick roof to its skull. A number of skulls have been discovered in North America, but only one complete skeleton has been dug up so far.

Scientists think that Pachycephalosaurus used its strong bony head when fighting for territory or a mate. The dinosaurs would charge at each other and bang their heads together with a mighty thump.

The skull protected the brain inside it. The skull roof could be up to 25 cm thick!

FACT FILE

- PAK-ee-KEF-al-oh-SAW-rus
- 'Thick-headed reptile'
- Lived in N. America

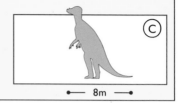

8m

Head-butting was a very important form of fighting. Males probably fought each other over territory and to impress females.

Its powerful legs helped the dinosaur to get a good run up to a head-butting charge.

Parasaurolophus

Parasaurolophus had the most amazing crest of any of the duckbilled dinosaurs. There were breathing tubes inside it, but it wasn't used as a snorkel because it was closed at the top! It could have been used to make honking sounds.

The shape and size of the crest varied, but some adults' crests were 1.8 metres long!

The small tough hooves show that duckbills could run for long distances over rough ground.

FACT FILE

- par-a-SAW-row-LOAF-us
- 'parallel-crested'
- Lived in N. America

Ⓒ

10m

Plateosaurus

Plateosaurus lived over 208 million years ago, during the Triassic, and was the first really big dinosaur. It was an ancestor of the huge plant-eaters Apatosaurus and Diplodocus. Plateosaurus was very common in Europe, and the remains of whole herds have often been found, killed by a flood.

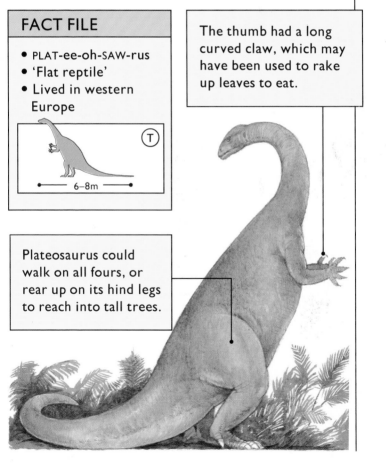

FACT FILE

- PLAT-ee-oh-SAW-rus
- 'Flat reptile'
- Lived in western Europe

6–8m (T)

The thumb had a long curved claw, which may have been used to rake up leaves to eat.

Plateosaurus could walk on all fours, or rear up on its hind legs to reach into tall trees.

Protoceratops

Protoceratops was one of the earliest horned dinosaurs. It only had a very low bump on its nose, unlike the sharp horns of its later relative Triceratops. The first bones were found in Mongolia in the 1920s. Whole nests were also discovered, with 20 or 30 eggs arranged in circles inside them.

FACT FILE

- pro-toe-SER-a-tops
- 'First horned-face'
- Lived in northern Asia

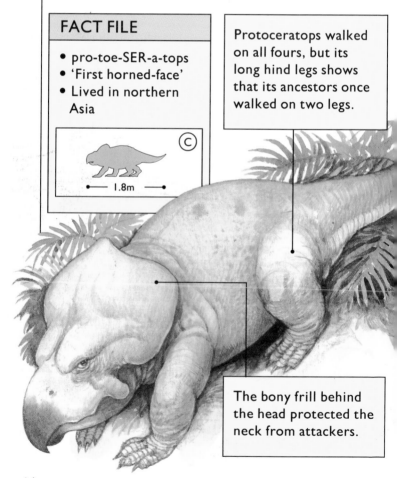

— 1.8m —

Protoceratops walked on all fours, but its long hind legs shows that its ancestors once walked on two legs.

The bony frill behind the head protected the neck from attackers.

Psittacosaurus

Psittacosaurus was the two-legged ancestor of Protoceratops. It didn't have the huge horns of its other relatives, Styracosaurus and Triceratops, but like all these dinosaurs it had a horny beak. Psittacosaurus was a plant-eater and its jaws were lined with dozens of teeth for grinding and chomping up its food.

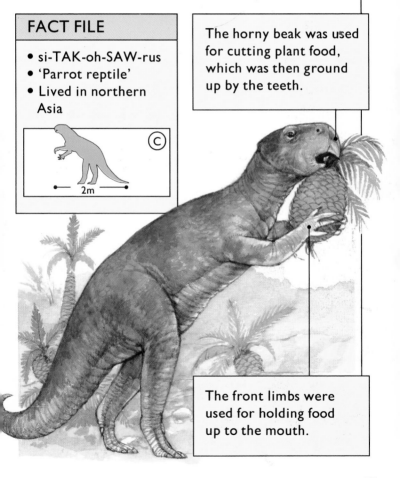

FACT FILE

- si-TAK-oh-SAW-rus
- 'Parrot reptile'
- Lived in northern Asia

© 2m

The horny beak was used for cutting plant food, which was then ground up by the teeth.

The front limbs were used for holding food up to the mouth.

Stegosaurus

Although Stegosaurus is one of the best-known dinosaurs, the plates on its back have always been a mystery – no one knows whether they should be in a single or a double row. This is because the plates weren't part of the backbone but grew in the skin instead, so they are always found separated from the main Stegosaurus skeleton.

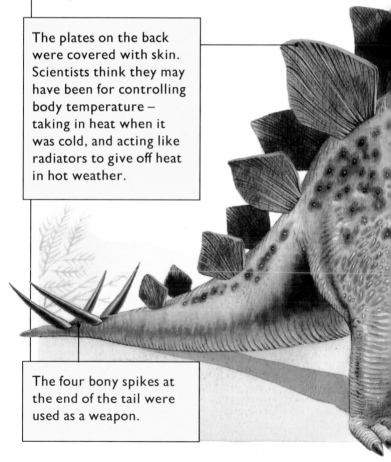

The plates on the back were covered with skin. Scientists think they may have been for controlling body temperature – taking in heat when it was cold, and acting like radiators to give off heat in hot weather.

The four bony spikes at the end of the tail were used as a weapon.

FACT FILE

- STEG-oh-SAW-rus
- 'Roofed reptile'
- Lived in North America

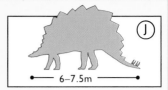

6–7.5m

Stegosaurus is often called the most stupid dinosaur because its skull contained a brain the size of a walnut!

Stenonychosaurus

Unlike Stegosaurus, Stenonychosaurus had a large brain and is thought to have been the cleverest of the dinosaurs!

Stenonychosaurus was related to Deinonychus and Velociraptor, and these three dinosaurs may have been similar to the ancestors of modern birds. They couldn't fly, though – they were all fast-moving land animals.

The slender tail was flicked from side to side to help with balance when running.

Stenonychosaurus' long fingers had curved claws which would have been useful for grasping and holding down prey. It probably ate lizards, frogs and small mammals.

Its large eyes helped Stenonychosaurus to see very clearly, even when hunting and chasing fast-moving prey.

Styracosaurus

Styracosaurus had more horns than any other dinosaur discovered so far – many more than its relative Triceratops. From the front this amazing display of horns must have looked quite terrifying, and may have even scared off an attacking Tyrannosaurus!

FACT FILE

- sty-RAK-oh-SAW-rus
- 'Spiked reptile'
- Lived in North America

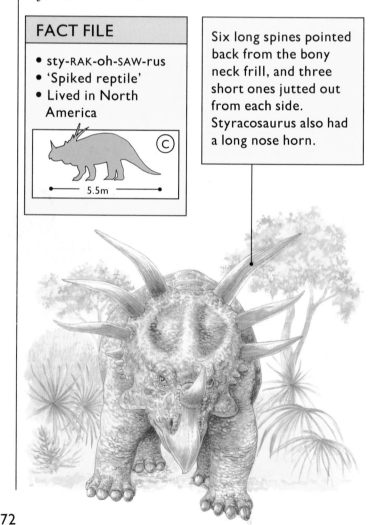

5.5m

Six long spines pointed back from the bony neck frill, and three short ones jutted out from each side. Styracosaurus also had a long nose horn.

Thecodontosaurus

Thecodontosaurus and its larger relative Plateosaurus were among the first dinosaurs to appear on Earth. Thecodontosaurus fossils have been found in caves and large cracks in the ground. The dinosaurs must have become trapped and died after falling into them.

Its long slender body must have allowed Thecodontosaurus to run quickly to escape its enemies.

Thecodontosaurus' hands were strong, with five fingers which were useful when picking leaves from trees to eat.

FACT FILE

- THEEK-oh-DON-to-SAW-rus
- 'Socket-toothed'
- Lived in England

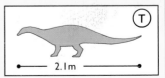

2.1m

Triceratops

Although nowadays more is known about Triceratops than about any other horned dinosaur, when fossils of its bony horns were first discovered in the 1880s they were thought to have come from a bison. Complete skulls were soon found, however, and these showed that Triceratops was far bigger and quite different from a bison!

FACT FILE

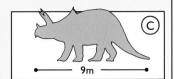

- try-SER-a-tops
- 'Three-horned face'
- Lived in North America

9m
©

The thick and heavy bony neck frill is part of the skull. It stopped fierce meat-eaters from trying to bite Tricera-tops around the neck.

The nose horn and the long pointed horns above the eyes must have been very effective at scaring off attacking dinosaurs.

Young Triceratops had to be protected by their fierce-looking parents from meat-eaters such as Tyrannosaurus.

Tyrannosaurus

Tyrannosaurus isn't only the most famous dinosaur, it was the biggest and most frightening meat-eater ever to have lived on Earth. Its head was 1.5 metres long – if Tyrannosaurus were alive today, a five-year old child would be able to stand inside its jaws. Tyrannosaurus' arms were tiny in comparison to the rest of its body, though. They weren't even long enough to reach its mouth!

Tyrannosaurus probably held down its prey with its huge feet while tearing at it with its teeth.

FACT FILE

- tie-RAN-oh-SAW-rus
- 'Tyrant reptile'
- Lived in North America

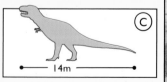

14m

The jaws were lined with sharp teeth which were the size and shape of steak knives – they could be as long as 18 cm!

Its tiny arms may have helped Tyrannosaurus to get up off the ground after sleeping.

77

Velociraptor

A close relative of Deinonychus, Velociraptor was another fierce hunter which terrorized the plant-eaters of its day. One Velociraptor skeleton was even found locked in struggle with a Protoceratops. They must have died while fighting. Velociraptor was holding on to Protoceratops' head shield, which had pierced its chest.

There was a long curved claw on one toe of each foot. Like Deinonychus, Velociraptor swung its foot down rapidly, tearing the flesh of its prey.

Zephyrosaurus

Only a skull and a few bones from the backbone of this dinosaur have been found, so we cannot be sure about its appearance. However, its ridged teeth were suitable for chomping at plants, and it may have looked rather like another plant-eater, Hypsilophodon.

Velociraptor's head was long and flat. It had about 30 curved teeth in its jaw.

FACT FILE

- vel-o-si-RAP-tor
- 'Fast thief'
- Lived in northern Asia

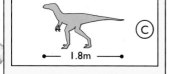

1.8m

FACT FILE

- zef-EYE-row-SAW-rus
- 'West-wind reptile'
- Lived in North America

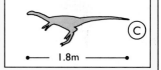

1.8m

AFTER THE DINOSAURS

The world must have seemed very empty after the dinosaurs died out at the end of the Cretaceous period. Scientists call the time since the dinosaurs' death to the present day the Cenozoic – the word *cenozoic* means 'new life'. Mammals have proved to be the most successful Cenozoic animals.

Palaeocene mammals were secretive. Many of the smaller ones slept during the day and came out to hunt during the cool of the night.

Pantolambda (1) and Barylambda (2) were pig-sized mammals which ate roots and reedy plants. Taeniolabis (3) was the size of a beaver. It ate nuts and fruit.

Plesiadapis (4), Planeto-therium (5) and Leptictis (6) were all insect-eaters. Plesiadapis could climb trees – its hands and feet were armed with strong claws. Planetotherium could stretch its body out to leap and glide from tree to tree.

The first age within the Cenozoic is called the Palaeocene. At the beginning of this time the only mammals were small insect-eaters. They gradually began trying out new ways of life, though, and larger plant- and meat-eating mammals evolved. Palaeocene forests were warm and jungle-like.

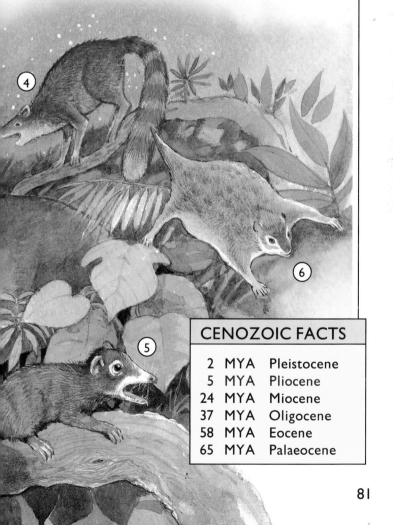

CENOZOIC FACTS

2	MYA	Pleistocene
5	MYA	Pliocene
24	MYA	Miocene
37	MYA	Oligocene
58	MYA	Eocene
65	MYA	Palaeocene

Mammal Ancestors

The ancestor of the modern horse appeared during Eocene times (58–37 million years ago). Hyracotherium was a dog-sized plant-eater which lived deep in the forests, eating leaves and creeping about quietly to avoid being caught by meat-eaters.

The Eocene meat-eaters were fairly terrifying. They included the huge flightless bird Diatryma and the mammals Andrewsarchus and Patrio-felis. Patriofelis was rather cat-like, but Andrewsarchus looked like a cross between a bear and a dog. It was a massive 5 metres long – its skull alone was nearly a metre long!

THE HISTORY OF THE HORSE

The first horse, Hyra-cotherium (1), had four toes instead of a hoof! It was tiny, compared to modern species (6). In between these two were Mesohippus (2) from the Oligocene, Merychippus (3) and Hypohippus (4) from the Miocene, and Pliohippus (5) from the Pliocene.

Uintatherium was the size of a modern rhinoceros. The tusks below its mouth could have been used for raking up roots and other plant food.

Andrewsarchus was four or five times the size of the largest lion alive today.

Patriofelis (above) was a hunter and probably stalked its prey. Phenacodus (left) was a plant-eater about the size of a sheep.

The ferocious meat-eating bird Diatryma was taller than a man!

The Grasslands Spread

The Earth's climate started getting cooler and drier during the Oligocene (37–24 million years ago), and open grasslands began taking over from thick forests. Many animals died out because they were more suited to life in the lush forests of earlier times.

Poebrotherium (1) was an early camel, which didn't have a hump. Cynodictis (2) was an early dog, Palaeolagus (3) was a rabbit, and Archaeotherium (4) was a pig. All these animals had strong legs and could run very quickly.

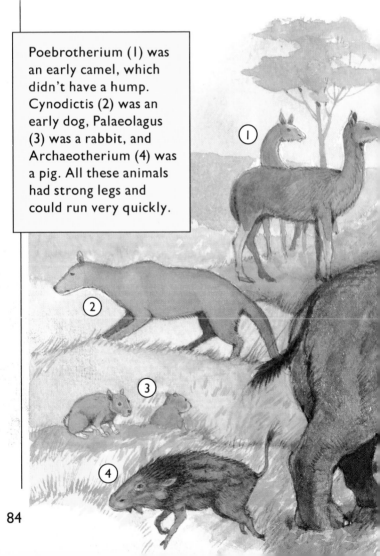

Among the new mammal groups were the ancestors of modern cats, dogs, pigs and camels. Many animals were fast runners – there were fewer trees to hide in, so plant-eaters had to be able to speed away from danger. And meat-eaters had to be able to catch them!

The sabre-toothed cat Hoplophoneus (5) looked like a tiger with long teeth. Brontotherium (6) was a plant-eater the size of a small elephant. Males probably used their catapult-shaped horns when fighting over territory or a mate.

The Age of Elephants

Although today there are just two types of elephant, the African and the Indian, during Miocene and Pliocene times (24–2 million years ago) there were all sorts of strange-looking species.

Like the other successful animals of their time, the early elephants were well suited to the weather and living conditions. The grasslands spread to cover most of the land on Earth during the Miocene and Pliocene. The climate was still warm, but in many parts of the world it became even drier than it had been during the Oligocene.

Animals that could live in very dry areas included the plant-eater Alticamelus (1). Nimravides (2) was a sabre-toothed cat. The beaver-like Epi-gaulus (3) died out as the grasslands spread.

Amphicyon (4) was a cross between a bear and a dog – it was about 3 m long and both fierce and fast enough to attack most plant-eaters of its day.

ALL ABOUT ELEPHANTS

The first elephants appeared during the Eocene, and by the Miocene they were a very varied group.

Their trunks and tusks came in all shapes and sizes – some were like shovels set into the elephant's lower jaws!

1 Gomphotherium
2 Deinotherium
3 Platybelodon

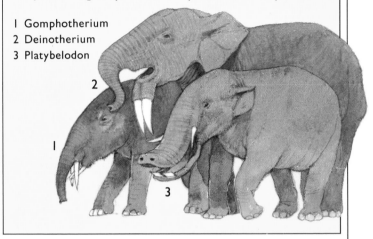

The Great Ice Age

About 2 million years ago, at the start of the Pleistocene, the Earth's climate became very cold. Snow and ice spread down from the North Pole, killing off many plants and animals. Some animals fled south, but others were suited to the freezing conditions and could live around the edges of the ice sheet.

The crow Corvus (above) was one of the few birds that could live around the edges of the ice sheet. Elasmotherium (right) was a huge woolly rhinoceros. Its nose horn alone could be as long as 2 metres!

The antlers of the giant Irish deer Megaloceros measured 2 metres across. Megaloceros was almost twice the size of a modern reindeer.

The ice-sheet animals included the woolly mammoth and rhinoceros, and the giant Irish deer. These animals were all kept warm by their heavy coats of fur and thick body fat. They were hunted by a new mammal species – human beings. Among our early relatives were the Neanderthal peoples of Europe.

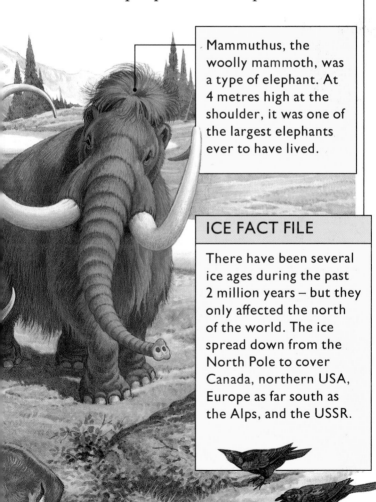

Mammuthus, the woolly mammoth, was a type of elephant. At 4 metres high at the shoulder, it was one of the largest elephants ever to have lived.

ICE FACT FILE

There have been several ice ages during the past 2 million years – but they only affected the north of the world. The ice spread down from the North Pole to cover Canada, northern USA, Europe as far south as the Alps, and the USSR.

USEFUL WORDS

Amphibians A group of cold-blooded animals which live in water and on land, and whose bodies change completely between young and adult forms. Amphibians living today include frogs, toads, newts and salamanders.

Anklyosaurs A group of dinosaurs which had a body armour of bony spines and knobs growing in their skin. Acantopholis and Ankylosaurus were both ankylosaurs.

Armoured dinosaurs See Anklyosaurs, Ceratopsians and Stegosaurs. The armoured dinosaurs were all plant-eaters.

Carnosaurs A group of large meat-eating dinosaurs which stood on their two hind legs. Allosaurus, Ceratosaurus, Megalosaurus and Tyrannosaurus were all carnosaurs.

Ceratopsians A group of armoured dinosaurs with beak-like mouths and horns on their heads. They included Styracosaurus and Triceratops.

Coelurosaurs This group of fast-moving hunters included the dinosaurs Coelophysis, Coelurus and Compsognathus.

Deinonychosaurs Deinonychus, Stenonychosaurus and Velociraptor were all deinonychosaurs – fierce meat-eating dinosaurs with vicious curved claws on their feet or hands.

Duckbilled dinosaurs See Hadrosaurs.

Evolution   The slow process of change and development in living things, which takes place over thousands and millions of years.

Extinction   When a plant or animal species dies and vanishes from the Earth forever, as the dinosaurs did 65 million years ago.

Fossil   The remains of ancient life, often turned to stone. Scientists have learnt about prehistoric life through studying fossils.

Hadrosaurs   A group of dinosaurs whose mouths were shaped like ducks' bills. They included Anatosaurus, Corythosaurus, Lambeosaurus, Maiasaura and Parasaurolophus. Many had crests on their heads. See also Ornithopods.

Ichthyosaurs   An extinct group of dolphin-like reptiles which lived in the seas at the same time as the dinosaurs ruled on land.

Mammals   A group of warm-blooded animals which feed their young on milk made in the mothers' bodies. Humans are mammals, as are cats and dogs, elephants and whales.

Ornithopods   A group of plant-eating dinosaurs which stood on their two hind legs. Ornithopods included the hadrosaurs, as well as Fabrosaurus, the hypsilophodonts (Dryosaurus, Hypsilophodon and Zephyrosaurus), the iguanodontids (Iguanodon, Muttaburrasaurus and Ouranosaurus), and the pachycephalosaur Pachycephalosaurus.

Palaeontologist A scientist who studies fossils and the history of living things.

Plesiosaurs An extinct group of long-necked reptiles which lived in the seas at the same time as the dinosaurs ruled on land.

Prehistoric Belonging to ancient times, thousands and millions of years ago.

Pterosaurs An extinct group of flying reptiles which were related to the dinosaurs. Pterosaurs were not birds, and their wings were covered in skin not feathers.

Reptiles A group of cold-blooded animals with scaly skins, which lay their eggs on land. Reptiles living today include alligators, crocodiles, lizards, snakes, tortoises and turtles.

Sauropods A group of large plant-eating dinosaurs with long necks and tails. Apatosaurus, Brachiosaurus, Cetiosaurus and Diplodocus were all sauropods.

Skeleton The bony framework which supports the bodies of amphibians, birds, fish, mammals and reptiles.

Species A unique or special type of animal or plant. All the members of a species look similar and can breed together. Apatosaurus and Brachiosaurus were two different species of dinosaur, for example.

Stegosaurs A group of dinosaurs which had a body armour of bony plates on their backs. Kentrosaurus and Stegosaurus were stegosaurs.

INDEX